HERBAL Tea

Your Practical Guide to Herbal Tea Remedies for Detox, Immunity, Stress Relief and Well-Being

Copyright © 2014 Ingrid Sen
All right reserved.

Disclaimer

The information in this book is not to be used as medical advice and is not meant to treat or diagnose medical problems. The information presented should be used in combination with guidance from your physician.

All rights reserved. No part of this publication or the information in it may be quoted from or reproduced in any form by means such as printing, scanning, photocopying or otherwise without prior written permission of the copyright holder.

Disclaimer and Terms of Use: Effort has been made to ensure that the information in this book is accurate and complete, however, the author and the publisher do not warrant the accuracy of the information, text and graphics contained within the book due to the rapidly changing nature of science, research, known and unknown facts and internet. The Author and the publisher do not hold any responsibility for errors, omissions or contrary interpretation of the subject matter herein. This book is presented solely for motivational and informational purposes only.

Introduction

People have been drinking tea for thousands of years. Initially discovered in ancient China, herbal tea began its long trajectory over the lands, bringing medicinal properties and hydration to people on every continent, in every corner of the world. Ancient Greek doctors utilized it to relieve everything from indigestion to labor pains. The ancient Egyptians thought of the herbs behind herbal teas as sometimes god-like, almost worthy of worship. The 17th century brought tea into the western world, when King Charles II married Catherine, a Portuguese princess, who declared that tea was the drink of royalty. At that time, herbs and natural medicines were still mainstays in the doctor handbag. But leaps and bounds in western medicine have brought the world further and further from the herbal tea's amazing benefits.

Herbal tea is one of the most calming, most relaxing elements to complete a cold winter day. It's an essential pick-me-up; it's wholesome and warming. People turn to it during gatherings, after work, over a good book—anytime they want to feel warmed and nourished. Because of herbal tea's amazing properties, the drink works to sooth stomach issues, calm anxieties, ease stress, halt the tremors of insomnia, and relieve cramps. In fact, many herbalists state that herbal tea brings many more benefits than a traditional vitamin pill. Herbal tea gives the body its essential ability to balance out hormones, to grow healthy cells, to boost youthful shine, and to gravitate toward a future of health.

Finding the right herbs can be difficult, of course, which is why this book outlines the most noteworthy bodily abnormalities and brings ready relief with step-by-step instructions and easy-to-follow recipes. A house full of herbs and a tea for every ailment is the ultimate goal of this book. Allow your medicine cabinet to fall to the hands of your kitchen herb supply. Find ready relief pulsing in your steaming cup of tea.

Note that this book brings the following:

1. Noteworthy benefits of all herbal teas.
2. Understanding of how to brew the perfect batch of herbal tea and how to drink that tea with utter sophistication (unless you're drinking it in sweatpants at home).

3. Recipes to cleanse your liver and your intestines to put you on a path to enhanced weight loss.

4. Recipes to relieve your stress and anxiety and decrease your level of the fight-or-flight hormone, cortisol.

5. Recipes that are fueled just-for-women to smooth the labor trajectory, reduce cramps, and balance out hormones.

6. And so many other herbal tea recipes to bring relief and elevate your life's vitality.

Table of Contents

Chapter 1: Benefits of Herbal Teas 9

Chapter 2: How to Make and Drink Tea with Easy Sophistication 21

Chapter 3: Detox Tea Recipes 27
Eastern Medicine Turmeric and Ginger Detox Tea 28
Dandelion Daydream Herbal Tea 30
Lucky Lemongrass Herbal Tea 31
Asian-Based Chrysanthemum Tea Recipe 33

Chapter 4: Antioxidant Tea Recipes 35
Cinnamon Dream Antioxidant-Boosting Herbal Tea 35
Honeybush Herbal Tea 37
Iced Dream Lavender Herbal Tea 39
Thyme to Boost Antioxidant Herbal Tea 41
Spearmint Delight Herbal Tea 42

Chapter 5: Immune-Boosting Tea Recipes 43
Rev Your Immune System with Spiced Goji Berry Herbal Tea 44
Ultimate Fighting Power Herbal Tea 46
The Elderberry Equation Herbal Tea 49
Immune-Boosting Sore Throat-Relieving Sage Herbal Tea 51

Chapter 6: Stress and Anxiety Relieving Tea Recipes 53
Ashwagandha Anxiety-Relieving Herbal Tea 54
Lemon Balm Stress Relief Herbal Tea 55
Hop Tea for Insomnia, Without the Beer 57
Citrus-Based Basil Calming Relief Herbal Tea 58

Chapter 7: Intestinal Relief Tea Recipes 59
IBS-Soothing Anise Herbal Tea 60
Chamomile Intestinal Relief 62
Fennel Relief Herbal Tea 64

Chapter 8: Herbal Teas Just For Women 65
Balance Your Hormones Alfalfa-Based Herbal Tea 65
Ok-For-Pregnancy Headache Relief Herbal Tea 68
The Anti Cramp Herbal Tea 70
The Laborious Process Herbal Tea 72

Conclusion 74

Chapter 1
BENEFITS OF HERBAL TEAS

Herbal tea is a mainstay. It's been around for thousands of years, winding its way generation after generation into the hearts and bellies of people all over the world. Some of them, now, are pausing over books, warming themselves with herbal tea during the page turns. Some of them are using tea as an excuse to catch up with old friends during the cold winter holidays, when the weather outside is blustery and the tea between both friends is warm and nourishing. They take sips between secrets. The ingredients pulsing in each cup of herbal tea brings something nearly magical, something hidden, that keeps us coming back for more, time and time again.

Alongside these warming, soothing opportunities, herbal tea administers a plethora of health benefits, bringing you comfort, relief, and ready calm in a sea of stress. It fights back against diseases, and it even boosts your immune system.

Herbal teas are known as tisanes. They offer an incredibly inexpensive way to fuel yourself with the appropriate herbs and spices that alleviate your pains and maximize your quality of life.

Note that scientists state that the benefits of tea come from its phytochemicals and polyphenols. They fuel the following amazing, life-affirming benefits.

1. Herbal tea fights against free radicals on a cellular level.

Free radicals are the elements that work against your DNA, alter it, and ultimately strap you with either dead cells or cancerous cells. Herbal tea, however, is high in something called oxygen radical absorbance capacity. Therefore, the herbal tea works to absorb the free radicals in your system and refute future disease.

2. Herbal tea boosts your cardiovascular health.

According to recent research, drinking tea renews your heart and decreases your risk of cardiovascular disease and heart attack.

3. Herbal tea helps you exercise longer and faster.

The antioxidants in many herbal teas can boost your bodily ability to turn to fat for fuel when you exercise. As such, you can lose weight and gain muscle as you exercise longer and faster.

4. Herbal tea refutes your intake of ultraviolent, dangerous sunrays.

It's essential to limit how many ultraviolent sunrays you soak up during the summer months. However, it's important to note that herbal tea has an extra "back up" ability to act as a sort of sunscreen.

5. Herbal tea helps you lose weight and sustain your weight loss.

According to a recent study, people who drank herbal tea on a daily basis had smaller waist sizes and a lower BMI than people who did not drink herbal tea (who had the same activity level). Furthermore, researchers state that herbal tea works to decrease your risk of developing metabolic syndrome. Note that metabolic syndrome increases your risk of artery disease, diabetes, and stroke.

But what are the ingredients pulsing beneath these benefits? Where do they come from?

Look to the following oft-utilized herbs and spices to better understand the benefits you'll reap with a hot cup of tea lodged between your hands. Note that you should avoid synthetic, artificially flavored "herbal" teas, as they do not have the enhanced qualities of the real herbs listed below.

GINGER

Ginger is a spice that's made from the rhizome of a ginger root plant. When you drink herbal ginger tea, you can help relieve nausea, cool your sharp joint pain in the case of both rheumatism and arthritis, and lower your bad cholesterol numbers. Furthermore, ginger tea can help rev your metabolism and help you lose a bit of weight along the way to greater health.

ELDERFLOWER

The Elder tree's beautiful flowers create this wonderful decongestant and cold-fighter. Furthermore, the flowers force the body to begin to sweat, allowing your overall body temperature to rise. It's noted by natural, homeopathic experts that viruses cannot readily grow in the temperature spike.

NETTLE

This English herb boosts your energy with its ready mineral count. It's pulsing with calcium, iron, and silica, and allows your body to produce extra bouts of red blood cells, which fuel your body with extra oxygen and wide-eyed energy. Note that silica and calcium help support your bone, teeth, and hair strength.

GREEN TEA

Japanese-based green tea leaves create overall tissue strength and therefore refute aging, disallowing your body's cells to sag. The green tea leaves contain an incredible level of antioxidants that fight against environmental and food pollutants that can hinder the vibrant nature of your healthy cells.

FENNEL

This Mediterranean-based herb allows your body to relax on both an exterior and interior level. As such, it works to refute colic and constipation and calm your stomach. Furthermore, fennel boosts your body's diuretic properties, allowing you to urinate more often and "re-boot" your organs. When your kidneys clean themselves out, your body produces clean, healthy, and youthful skin production.

THYME

Another Mediterranean-based herb, Thyme fights colds and flus with its volatile cellular oils. When thyme is formulated into herbal teas, your chest works to cleanse and clear out on your way to better health and comfort.

PEPPERMINT

Peppermint is a perfect anti-nausea herb that boosts gall bladder-based bile production. As such, the fat that's causing nausea in your body is broken down easily and allowed to pass through your system, leaving you with ready relief.

ST. JOHN'S WORT

This European-based yellow flower brings anti-depression elements and can work to reverse Seasonal Affective Disorder. It's noted, on a scientific level, that this St. John's Wort, when formulated into a tea, can actually raise serotonin—the happy chemical—in the brain.

Chapter 2
HOW TO MAKE AND DRINK TEA WITH EASY SOPHISTICATION

The Essential Rules for Making the Perfect Cup of Tea

When making your herbal tea, it's important to learn to be diligent and precise. After all, you're working to better your health with the most ancient technique available: herbal tea. You must withhold the centuries-old tradition of creating this work-of-art, masterpiece herbal tea

Look to the following tips.

1. Always brew your tea for longer than three minutes.

When you bring your herbs and your boiling water together, you must let them play together for longer than you might like. The respectable number is three minutes. However, if you want to reap the benefits of the perfect cup of herbal tea, you'll want to wait a bit longer. Plus, you'll want to allow the tea to cool down to healthful, appropriate temperatures.

2. Always strain your herbal tea or take the tea bag out.

Don't leave your tea bag in your tea, and further don't drink your tea with the herbs in it! The bag becomes messy, and the herbs land in your teeth and create later social problems. Plus, the tea simply tastes better if you allow it to steep for only a specific amount of time.

3. Store your tea leaves or your herbs in an airtight container, far away from things like soap, cheese, or other spices. The herbs and leaves can "take on" the aroma of these other things and become tainted.

4. Always utilize teapots that are made of earthenware, china, or stainless steel. Don't bother with the enamel or tin pots.

5. Remember always that the water you boil will be the water that creates your herbal tea. Thusly, you must utilize good, clean, healthful water to reap all the benefits of your herbs. Note that if you want to utilize tap water, you should always allow it to "run" through the faucet, cold, for at least ten seconds before pouring it into your saucepan or tea kettle.

How to Drink Tea with Easy Sophistication

Have you ever wondered how you're "supposed" to drink tea, according to the ancient line of tea drinkers throughout the world? If you find yourself in a social setting, it's essential that you learn how to drink tea appropriately to look like a mature, well-rounded, hydrated person.

First of all, don't hold your teacup with your pinky out. Oftentimes, this is actually considered rude! Instead, position your index finger inside the handle of your teacup while positioning your thumb on the top of the handle for security. Your third finger should have the bottom of the handle.

Hundreds of years ago, it was appropriate to pour the milk (if you choose to drink your herbal tea with milk) into the teacup prior to pouring the tea. This was a practical choice, done in order to prevent teacups from cracking. Today, it's essential that you pour the milk after the tea in order not to use too much milk.

When you stir your tea, it's important to be mindful of where your spoon lands. Don't clink it against the side of your cup. After you're done stirring, place the spoon on the saucer, behind your cup, on the right side of the handle. Don't even think about sipping from your spoon.

When you're sitting at a table alongside other tea drinkers, it's important that you don't lift up your saucer as you drink. Leave the plate on the table. Note that this is different than when you're walking and talking with your saucer. As you take a drink, no matter if you're seated or standing, it's important that you keep your eyes down as you drink to pay attention to what you're doing.

Good luck drinking tea with others! Alternately, just stay home with your favorite book, your favorite pair of slippers, and the heater turned up to have a calm, lazy afternoon to yourself. Drink your tea with your pinky out, for all I care.

Drink Tea Safely and Appropriately

The long-purported benefits of herbal tea can cause us to turn to it, over and over again, for comfort and a ready boost of health. However, it's essential to drink tea in an appropriate manner to fuel greater safety and provide an environment for the benefits to take hold.

Note always to allow your tea to cool to hot from boiling before even drinking it. When you drink super-hot beverages daily, you'll boost your risk of having esophageal cancer. Therefore, you should first allow your beverage to cool at least fifteen minutes. Note that you can always drink your tea cold if you're especially worried about the dangers of hot tea.

Furthermore, if you are pregnant or have unique health difficulties, always read and ask your doctor about each of the purported herbs in this book. Oftentimes, for example, pregnant women shouldn't have certain herbs. Always keep your personal safety in mind when proceeding.

Chapter 3
DETOX TEA RECIPES

Detox herbal teas provide a way for you to detox your body from environmental and food-based pollutants. The herbal tea allows you to detox your liver, lose a bit of weight, boost your energy, and bring an overall cleanse to your cells that can make you look younger and fresher.

Look to the following top 7 herbs that create this detox effect, and then turn to the following tea recipes in order to cleanse yourself from the inside out.

1. Goji berries
2. Chrysanthemum flowers
3. Oolong Leaf
4. Dandelion Leaf
5. Rose Flower
6. Pu'er Leaf
7. Lemongrass

Eastern Medicine Turmeric and Ginger Detox Tea

This ginger and turmeric-based herbal tea is an essential start to your detox regime. Ginger is pulsing with a whirlwind of medicinal properties. It offers anti-inflammatory and antioxidant elements that reduce your affinity for disease. Furthermore, it cleanses your liver, your intestines, and your body on a cellular level to provide ready relief.

Turmeric, an Indian herb that works alongside ginger, is a natural liver cleanser. When you cleanse your liver, you provide an easy route for your body to regulate its acidity levels. When your body's acidity levels are too high, you are unable to lose weight and you put yourself at greater risk of developing diseases.

Ingredients:

2-inch piece ginger root
½ tsp. cayenne pepper
2-inch piece turmeric root
1 tsp. vanilla stevia
juice from 3 lemons
1 3/4 quarts water

Directions:

Begin by bringing together ginger root, turmeric root, and the lemons in a juicer. Juice the ingredients together well.

Next bring the juiced mixture into a pitcher with the water and the vanilla stevia. Dash in the cayenne pepper, and stir the ingredients well. Allow the tea to rest for fifteen minutes, assimilating the taste and medicinal properties throughout the liquid.

Enjoy the tea at room temperature. Note that this tea is pretty spicy; it'll fight back.

Dandelion Daydream Herbal Tea

Note that dandelion leaves and roots are classic homeopathic utilizations, bringing vitamin A, iron, potassium, and calcium. Furthermore, it relieves your kidneys and your liver from multiple toxins.

Ingredients:
5 tbsp. dried dandelion root
11 tbsp. fresh dandelion leaves
4 cups boiling water

Directions:
Begin by boiling the water and then bringing the dried dandelion root and the dandelion leaves together in the boiling hot water. Stir for a moment before allowing it to sit and steep for approximately five minutes. Afterwards, filter out the water and drink the tea warm.
Enjoy.

Lucky Lemongrass Herbal Tea

Lemongrass offers a plethora of benefits that can ultimately assist in creating an overall body detox. Furthermore, it can reduce your indigestion and regulate your intestines.

Lemongrass tea further boosts your sense of calm. It can fight insomnia while boosting your mood and reverting your depressive symptoms. It acts as a vitamin A booster, allowing your skin to look youthful and bright.

Note that you should avoid the lemongrass herbal tea if you are pregnant or are allergic to many such "outdoor" grasses.

Ingredients:
2 tbsp. dried lemongrass leaves
2 cups boiling water
optional 1 tsp. of honey

Directions:
Begin by boiling water. Afterwards, pour the boiling water over the lemongrass leaves and allow the leaves to steep for five minutes. Strain the tea and sweeten it with a bit of honey, if you so choose.

Drink the lemongrass tea after meals in order to cleanse your system of the heavy fats and proteins.

Enjoy.

Asian-Based Chrysanthemum Tea Recipe

This Chinese-based tea is an essential path to detoxify your body and allow yourself to lose weight.

Ingredients:
1 cup dried white chrysanthemum flowers
3 tbsp. honey
½ tsp. dried Goji berries
3 ½ cups boiling water

Directions:
Begin by completely rinsing off both the flowers and the Goji berries in cold water. Afterwards, position both the berries and the flowers in the teapot.

To the side, bring the water to a boil. After it begins boiling, pour the water into the teapot and allow both the berries and the flowers to steep for approximately seven minutes. At this time, add the honey to taste, stirring as you pour.

Now, you have two options. You can either serve the tea hot or cold. Serve the tea hot, now. Alternately, allow the tea to cool prior to straining the tea. Position the strained tea in a refrigerator-friendly pitcher and allow it to chill prior to serving.

Enjoy!

Chapter 4
ANTIOXIDANT TEA RECIPES

Cinnamon Dream Antioxidant-Boosting Herbal Tea

Cinnamon is an ingredient you can find anywhere. It's a main ingredient in everything from your grandma's cookies to your chemically-altered pop tarts. Cinnamon is one of the oldest known spices in the world. Ancient Chinese medical practitioners turned to this herb for its antioxidant benefits. It was shown to reduce interior inflammation and even to fight colds and flus.

Ingredients:
1 cinnamon stick (or 1 tsp. of cinnamon)
1 cup boiling water
1 slice lemon

Directions:

If you've chosen to work with a cinnamon stick, you must break it down at this time and position the pieces in your teacup. Alternately, pour the ground cinnamon into your teacup.

To the side, boil the water. Pour the boiling water over your cinnamon and allow the cinnamon to steep for ten minutes. If you've chosen to utilize cinnamon sticks, remove the cinnamon pieces.

At this time, add the honey to the cinnamon to sweeten it up. Toss the piece of lemon into the mix and enjoy your herbal, antioxidant-revving cinnamon tea.

Honeybush Herbal Tea

Honeybush tea is in the rooibos family tree, a South African-based herbal assortment that brings a variety of benefits. Its antioxidant properties allow your body to reduce its cancer risks. Furthermore, one of its most essential antioxidants, Chysoeriol, works to boost your overall heart health, improve your circulation, and lower your bad cholesterol levels.

Furthermore, honeybush works to relieve many skin conditions, like acne, psoriasis, and eczema. It creates a sort of interior calm in you, as well, that can halt your sense of anxiety and improve your quality of life.

Ingredients:
1 tbsp. dried honeybush leaves
1 cup boiling water
½ tsp. honey

Directions:

Begin by pouring the dried honeybush leaves into your teacup. To the side, boil your water. After it begins boiling, pour the water over the leaves. Allow the leaves to steep for approximately ten minutes. Afterwards, strain the tea and add the honey to bring out the "honey" layer of the honeybush leaves.

Enjoy the tea warm.

Iced Dream Lavender Herbal Tea

Lavender is well-known for its luxurious smell. However, lavender further brings you an enhanced ability to relax in the face of stress, to kill bodily pathogens, and to fight cancer-causing free radicals. The strong force of antioxidants become a second line of command against anything attacking the youthfulness and vitality of your body.

Ingredients:
4 bags of green tea
1 tsp. dried lavender or 2 tsp. fresh lavender blossoms
1 quart boiling water

Directions:
Begin by pouring the water into the saucepan and heating it on medium-high until it begins to simmer. At the point of simmering, remove the

water from the heat and add the lavender and the tea to the water.

Allow the lavender and the tea to steep for a full seven minutes. Strain the tea into a refrigerator-proof pitcher and allow it to cool completely.

Next, pour the mixture into glasses filled with ice and enjoy the antioxidant-rich iced tea.

Thyme to Boost Antioxidant Herbal Tea

Thyme contains many antioxidants as well as cold and flu-fighting elements to reduce symptoms. Note that a ready intake of thyme tea can reduce your risk of serious heart disease, diabetes, and even everyday ailments, like anxiety or the cold.

Ingredients:
1 inch grated ginger
1 tsp. dried thyme
1 tsp. dried sage
1 tbsp. honey
1 cup boiling water

Directions:
Position the above herbs in your teacup. To the side, boil the water. Pour the water into your teacup and allow the ingredients to steep for approximately seven minutes.

Next, strain the teacup water and utilize a bit of honey to brighten the flavor. Enjoy the antioxidant-rich tea.

Spearmint Delight Herbal Tea

Spearmint, peppermint's ever-incredible cousin, has many antioxidant-based benefits. It allows you to ward off serious stomach problems, and it further boosts your immune system, paving the way for a healthy road ahead.

Ingredients:
4 stalks of spearmint
3 ½ cups boiling water
1 tbsp. honey

Directions:
Begin by allowing the 3 ½ cups of water to boil on the stovetop.

To the side, crush the spearmint a bit in your fingers before depositing it into a teapot. Pour the boiling water over the spearmint. Cover the teapot with its lid and allow the spearmint to steep for a full seven minutes.

At this time, strain the tea, and enjoy the drink warm.

Chapter 5
IMMUNE-BOOSTING TEA RECIPES

In those desperate winter months, it's essential that you boost your immune system to ward off serious diseases, like the flu and the common cold. Note that when your immune system isn't working at top-speed, you experience things like muscle weakness, tiredness, inflammation, infection, and allergic reactions. Turn to the following herbal teas in order to boost your immune system, feel strong, and build a powerful bodily structure to ward off future diseases.

Rev Your Immune System with Spiced Goji Berry Herbal Tea

Goji berries, mentioned in a previous chapter, have vitamin C benefits that can help you fight against any vengeful bacterium or viruses currently pulsing in your body. The Goji berry antioxidants further help your body to decrease the free radical damage in your body—the damage that can ultimately lead to cancer and other dangerous diseases.

Ingredients:
½ cup Goji berries
2 tsp. grated ginger root
5 cloves
juice from ½ lemon
1 tbsp. honey
3 3-inch strips of orange peel
2 ½ cup water

Directions:

Begin by bringing the water to a boil in a saucepan or a teapot. After it begins to boil, add the ginger, orange peels, lemon juice, and the cloves. Stir well, and allow the ingredient flavors to pulse in the water for about fifteen minutes. (If you want to keep your tea extra hot, you can leave the burner on low as this occurs.)

After fifteen minutes, strain the created tea into two teacups. Add half a cup of Goji berries to each teacup, and add ½ tbsp. of honey to each cup, as well.

Enjoy.

Ultimate Fighting Power Herbal Tea

This recipe contains every herb your body requires to heal itself and make you feel well again. It contains, for one, elderberries, which are vibrant with vitamin A, B, and C. Furthermore, the elderberries have been utilized for centuries to take a stand against colds and flus.

Furthermore, this ultimate fighting power herbal tea contains elderflowers, which work to cleanse your sinuses and keep you ever inhaling and exhaling.

Turn to this fighting power herbal tea for chamomile, rose hips, and astragulus, as well, all herbs that calm your interior bodily cells, ease inflammation, and help to retain your body's energy to keep fighting the good fight.

The Echinacea purpurea herb, on the other hand, offers the secret weapon of herb fighting power. It actually enhances your cellular ability to fight back against infection. It contains the trifecta of anti-fungal, anti-bacterial, and anti-viral properties.

This Ultimate Fighting Power Herbal Tea blend is bright and colorful—perfect to pull out in the middle of a gray, winter afternoon.

Ingredients:
1 tsp. elderflowers
1 tsp. elderberries
1 tsp. rose hips
1 tsp. chamomile
1 tsp. Echinacea
1 tsp. astragulus
1 cup boiling water

Directions:
Begin by bringing the above herbs together, stirring well, in a large bowl or container. (Note that you can continually store this herb mix in your cupboard for future uses, if you want to make each cup one at a time.)

When you wish to drink your herbal tea, simply portion out 1 tsp. of the mixture into a teacup. To the side, boil one cup of water on the stovetop.

Next, pour the hot water over the herbs. Allow the herbs to steep for a full ten minutes before straining out the herbs and enjoying the warm tea. Add honey, if you so please, for an electrifying sweetener.

Enjoy!

The Elderberry Equation Herbal Tea

Elderberry can be utilized either to boost your immune system to avoid the flu or to fight back against your symptoms mid-illness. Note that elderberries are very delicious. When they're utilized with these mulling spices, the result brings an entirely pleasant, immune-boosting result.

Ingredients:
1 cinnamon stick
2 tbsp. dried elderberries
3 cloves
½ tsp. honey
2 cups water

Directions:
Begin by positioning the above ingredients—cinnamon stick, dried elderberries, cloves, and

the water—not the honey—into a saucepan. Allow the mixture to simmer for approximately thirty minutes.

At this time, strain the tea into a teacup, and add the honey to sweeten the flavor. Enjoy.

Immune-Boosting Sore Throat-Relieving Sage Herbal Tea

When sage and hot water come together, the result is an ultimate healing effect in your throat. Furthermore, spearmint is packed with other benefits, including antioxidants, vitamins, and nutrients that work to reduce nausea, headaches, feelings of indigestion, sore throat, and cramps.

Further research notes that sage has a surprising ability to treat something called "hirutism," which is a case of abnormal hair growth as a result of strange, irregular hormones in women. Sage tea can actually reduce the hormonal level of androgens which can reduce the growth of hair on the woman's stomach, breasts, and face. (Generally speaking, hirutism occurs as a result of serious life stressors.)

Look to the following sage herbal tea recipe for details.

Ingredients:
6 dried sage leaves
1 liter boiling water

Directions:

Begin by boiling 1 liter of water on the stovetop. Position the dried sage leaves inside of a 1 liter mason jar (or heat-ready pitcher) and pour the boiling water overtop the leaves. Position the mason jar lid over the leaves and allow the leaves to steep for fifteen minutes.

Utilize the created tea in order to either gargle to ease your scratchy, cold-ridden throat or simply to drink slowly to cool your interior inflammation. Note that you should be drinking approximately four cups of sage per day in order to relieve your aches and pains. Make sure you drink it appropriately so that it reaches into the back, dark caveats of your throat. Try to swirl it a bit before drinking.

Chapter 6
STRESS AND ANXIETY RELIEVING TEA RECIPES

Our daily lives administer a good deal of stress and anxiety. Some of us handle it better than others; regardless, we all need a way to calm ourselves after a long day, to ease our levels of cortisol, and help reduce our risk of inflammation, which can result with too much stress and anxiety coursing through our veins.

Turn to the following natural stress and anxiety-relieving herbal teas.

Ashwagandha Anxiety-Relieving Herbal Tea

This 4,000 year old herb has been utilized from Pakistan to India in order to bring bodily health and a reduced feeling of stress.

Ingredients:
1 tsp. ashwagandha, found as a whole root powder
1 cup boiling water
½ tsp. honey

Directions:
Begin by bringing the ashwagandha whole root powder into your teacup. To the side, boil the one cup of water. Pour the water over the whole root powder, and position a lid over the tea cup. Allow the herb to steep for fifteen minutes before straining the herb. Pour a bit of honey into the water to sweeten it just enough. Drink it all throughout the evening to calm yourself down.

Lemon Balm Stress Relief Herbal Tea

Lemon balm is a mint-based medicinal herb first-used by the ancient Greeks. It's been utilized both historically and today for stress and anxiety relief. The research of the lemon balm backs up its stress relief strength. It decreases the level of cortisol, the fight-or-flight hormone, in your bloodstream and boosts production of GABA, which is something anti-anxiety medications work to do utilizing chemicals.

The other ingredients in this tea are pulsing with benefits, as well. Rosehip brings an extra bout of vitamin C, which can relieve your cold and flu symptoms. Furthermore, oatstraw works to ease anxiety alongside the lemon balm. It contains many other minerals, vitamin B, and calcium, as well. Lavender, bringing that extra dose of good smells, is an essential herb to relieve anxiety and depression.

Ingredients:

1 tbsp. dried oatstraw

1 ½ tbsp. dried lemon balm

1 tsp. dried orange peel

2 tsp. dried rosehips

½ tsp. dried lavender

Directions:

Begin by bringing the above herbs together in a small mixing bowl. Stir them together and then position them in a mason jar.

When you wish to make a tea, pour 1 tsp. of the herbs into your teacup. Boil one cup of water to the side, and pour the water over the herbs. Cover the tea cup and allow the herbs to steep for twenty minutes. Strain the tea before sweetening it, if you please, with a bit of honey.

Enjoy!

Hop Tea for Insomnia, Without the Beer

Did you know there was once a utilization for hops that didn't include extra bouts of calories, huge burps, and slurred speech?

Hop tea dates back to ancient Greece and Rome. It can heal your insomnia, boost your appetite, bring ready relief to your joint pain, and soothe your muscle spasms. Drink it before you go to bed to fall asleep more quickly.

Ingredients:
1 ounce dried hops
1 quart boiling water

Directions:
Begin by bringing 1 ounce of the dried hops into a 1-quart container. To the side, boil one quart of water. Pour the water over the hops, and cover the pitcher. Allow the herbs to steep for approximately twenty minutes. Strain the tea, next, and drink it either hot or cold.

Enjoy this non-beer, insomnia-reducing hop tea.

Citrus-Based Basil Calming Relief Herbal Tea

Basil works to reduce serious anxiety distress. It further reduces your cortisol levels, which ultimately decreases your risk of interior inflammation. It counteracts both stress and depression and can work to give you a renewed sense of vitality and life.

Ingredients:
1 tbsp. grated lemon zest
2 ½ tbsp. chopped, fresh basil leaves
1 ½ tsp. black tea leaves
2 cups water

Directions:
Begin by bringing the water to a boil in a small saucepan. After it begins to boil, remove the water from the heat and add the lemon zest, the basil, and the black tea leaves to the saucepan. Cover the saucepan and allow the tea to steep for seven minutes. Strain the tea, and serve the tea warm, either with honey or without. Enjoy.

Chapter 7
INTESTINAL RELIEF TEA RECIPES

Intestinal pain can deplete your quality of life in an instant. Whether it's a one-day issue or a common problem, you must look to the following herbal tea recipes in order to relieve your indigestion, your intestinal cramps, and your gas.

IBS-Soothing Anise Herbal Tea

This licorice-flavored, Middle Eastern-based anise tea brings relief to your stomachaches, bloating, and gas. Furthermore, it works as a laxative, allowing you to cleanse your system and "start over."

Ingredients:
2 tsp. dried anise leaves or 2 tsp. whole anise seeds
2 ½ cups boiling water
2 black tea bags

Directions:
Begin by bringing one cup of water into one saucepan along with either the anise seeds or the anise leaves.

To the side, boil the remaining one and a half cups of water. After it's finished boiling, add the tea bags and steep them for approximately seven minutes.

Strain the anise leaf or anise seed water into the pot with the tea bags. Remove the tea bags, and serve the tea warm. Add honey or lemon to the tea for enhanced flavor, if you so choose.

Chamomile Intestinal Relief

The chamomile plant offers the chamomile flowers, brewed often for its anxiety relieving effects, its anti-spasmodic effects, and its allowance of reduced inflammation on a cellular level. Note that anxiety, inflammation, and spasms all occur on an intestinal and stomach level and cause pain. The chamomile can halt this pain in its tracks and get you on the path to better health.

Interestingly enough, ancient Egyptians turned to chamomile for its medicinal properties, believing the plant to be sacred and god-like. A Greek physician named Dioscorides further turned to chamomile in order to relieve liver disorders, anxiety, and serious stomach and intestinal disorders.

Ingredients:

1 tsp. dried chamomile flowers
1 cup boiled water
½ tsp. cinnamon

Directions:

Begin by boiling the water in a saucepan or teapot. Pour the dried chamomile flowers into a teacup, and then pour the water overtop the flowers. Place a top on the teacup and allow the flowers to steep for ten minutes. Strain the tea, and drink the tea slowly to relieve your gastrointestinal pain. Enjoy.

Fennel Relief Herbal Tea

Fennel tea has a mild laxative effect and brings an antispasmodic element, both of which work to relieve digestion discomfort. Furthermore, it can reduce your hunger pains and put you on a better diet track.

Ingredients:
1 tsp. fennel seeds
1 cup water

Directions:
Begin by briefly grinding the fennel seeds with a mortar and pestle just before brewing them.

Boil the water. Bring the tsp. of fennel seeds into your teacup, and pour the water overtop. Place a lid over the teacup, and allow the seeds to steep for ten minutes. Strain the tea and serve it warm.

Enjoy before meals to both boost your digestion and reduce your hunger.

Chapter 8
HERBAL TEAS JUST FOR WOMEN

Balance Your Hormones Alfalfa-Based Herbal Tea

As the title suggests, this herbal tea balances your hormone. It further works to boost your fertility, especially when you consume it regularly. Note that the alfalfa is a known estrogen-booster, while the lemon balm boosts your spirits, the raspberry leaf acts as a uterine tonic, and the vitex acts as an overall hormonal balancer.

Note that this recipe creates a large batch of the mixed herbs together that you can store in a large ball jar between uses. This tea is best utilized once or twice per day.

Ingredients:

½ cup alfalfa
½ cup nettle
½ cup red clover leaf
½ cup yarrow
½ cup fennel seed
½ cup lemon balm
½ cup orange peel
½ cup vitex
½ cup hibiscus flowers
½ cup oatstraw
½ cup peppermint

Directions:

Bring the above ingredients together in a large mixing bowl. Stir the ingredients well with a wooden spoon before pouring the mixture into a large mason jar to store in a cool, dry location.

When you wish to brew your tea, simply position the following ingredients together:

1 tsp. of the dried herbal mixture
1 cup boiling water

Allow the cup of water to boil. Bring the tsp. of herbs into your teacup, and then pour the water overtop of the herbs. Cover the cup and allow the herbs to steep for approximately fifteen minutes. Strain the water, and sweeten your tea, if you like, with either stevia or honey.

Drink the tea to balance your hormones and create a well-rounded, natural life.

Ok-For-Pregnancy Headache Relief Herbal Tea

When you're pregnant, many medications do not suit you. After all, you're trying to give all your nutrients to the baby growing inside of you. Therefore, this headache, which could be a result of stress, the weather, or overarching fatigue, should be quelled utilizing herbs like skullcap, chamomile, and lavender. Look to the following recipe to better understand this headache relief herbal tea.

Ingredients:
1 tsp. dried skullcap
1 tsp. dried chamomile
1 tsp. dried lemon balm
1 tsp. dried lemon peel
1 tsp. dried lavender

Directions:
Bring the above ingredients together in a small mixing bowl, and stir them together utilizing a wooden spoon. Store the mixture in a small mason jar.

When you're ready to drink the tea, simply position 1 tsp. of the mixed herbs into your teacup. To the side, boil one cup of water. Pour the water over the herbs and allow them to steep for fifteen minutes. Enjoy the tea every time you feel a headache creeping in. Sweeten it utilizing honey or stevia.

The Anti Cramp Herbal Tea

Turmeric, the ancient Indian herb, can be utilized for serious menstrual cramps and heavy bleeding. The science behind it looks like this:

When you have your menstrual cycle, your hormones called progesterone and estrogen can become imbalanced. When this occurs, your uterine lining builds up faster and stronger, leading to even more blood to be shed during the period. However, turmeric actually works to both halt this excessive building and stop the production of prostaglandin, which reduces your cramp pain.

As a result of this tea, you should have a steadier flow that is not too heavy. You should not feel too fatigued as a result of your period, and your cramp pain should be minimal.

Ingredients:
½ tsp. turmeric
½ tsp. ginger
1 tsp. cinnamon
1 cup coconut milk
1 tsp. honey

Directions:

Begin by heating the coconut milk in a saucepan over medium heat. After it begins to steam, add the honey and the spices. Stir the tea well, and serve it warm.

Enjoy!

The Laborious Process Herbal Tea

When you're in the labor process, you'll want to stay hydrated and decrease your level of pain. As such, you should turn to this incredible mixture of herbs.

Raspberry leaf brings uterine tonic abilities throughout your labor, which can ultimately result in the easy delivery of the placenta.

Chamomile, also utilized in this herbal recipe, relieves your bodily tension and thus allows you to cruise through the pain waves.

The nettle tea works to prevent postpartum hemorrhage. It further increases your body's ability to create breast milk. As such, you should drink it both throughout pregnancy and throughout labor in order to bring this milk in rapidly.

Ingredients:
1 tsp. dried red raspberry leaves
1 tsp. dried nettle
1 tsp. dried chamomile

Directions:

Stir the above herbs together in a small mixing bowl, and pour them together into a mason jar that's ready for your first hours of labor (pre-hospital). When you feel the process beginning, turn to the creation of this tea to keep your mind calm. Take 1 ounce of the dried leaves and position it in a 1-quart jar. To the side, boil 1 quart of water. Pour the water into the 1-quart jar, position the lid overtop, and then allow it to steep for thirty minutes.

Drink the tea either hot or cold, and calm yourself in the hours before your baby is born. You can sweeten the tea with honey, if you like.

Conclusion

Herbal tea brings a plethora of ancient-prescribed benefits to help ease your anxiety, reduce your indigestion, get you through the waves of nausea and stress of labor, allow you to balance your hormones to lose weight more readily, reduce your headaches, and live a vital, youthful life. Do not allow yourself to take the "easy" route of chemically-altered medications, and turn back to the earth. Herbal teas offer so much more than medicinal relief, as well. They offer companionship in the wake of an "herbal tea" party. They offer aromatherapy. They offer a time of solace from the busy day.

Allow herbal teas and the medicinal benefits of the earth to change your life.

Printed in Great Britain
by Amazon